21st Century Junior Library

WORKING AT A PARK

by Katie Marsico

CHERRY LAKE PUBLISHING * ANN ARBOR, MICHIGAN

Published in the United States of America by Cherry Lake Publishing
Ann Arbor, Michigan
www.cherrylakepublishing.com

Content Adviser: Sharon Castle, PhD, Associate Professor of Elementary Social Studies,
George Mason University, Fairfax, VA

Reading Consultant: Cecilia Minden-Cupp, PhD, Literacy Specialist and Author

Photo Credits: Page 4, ©Serghei Starus, used under license from Shutterstock, Inc.; cover and page
6, ©iofoto, used under license from Shutterstock, Inc.; cover and page 8, ©iStockphoto.com/Ljupco;
page 10, ©iStockphoto.com/hartemink; cover and page 12, ©Edwin Verin, used under license from
Shutterstock, Inc.; page 14, ©Jochen Tack/Alamy; page 16, ©Urikiri-Shashin-Kan/Alamy; page 18,
©prism_68, used under license from Shutterstock, Inc.; cover and page 20, ©Jaimie Duplass, used
under license from Shutterstock, Inc.

LIBRARY OF CONGRESS CATALOGING-IN-PUBLICATION DATA
Marsico, Katie, 1980–
  Working at a park / by Katie Marsico.
       p. cm.
  Includes index.
  ISBN-13: 978-1-60279-267-8
  ISBN-10: 1-60279-267-4
  1. Parks—Juvenile literature. 2. Parks—Employees—Juvenile literature.
  I. Title.
  SB481.3.M37 2009
  363.6'8023—dc22   2008008304

Cherry Lake Publishing would like to acknowledge the work of
The Partnership for 21st Century Skills.
Please visit www.21stcenturyskills.org for more information.

CONTENTS

Park workers sometimes wear gloves to protect their hands.

What Is a Park?

You have just finished playing on the slide. There are still a few minutes before your softball game starts. Do you want to watch the **groundskeeper** plant flowers while you wait? He is one of the workers you see at the park. Each worker wants you to have fun and enjoy yourself.

Bring a blanket to sit on when you have a picnic in a park.

A park is where people go to play or spend time outdoors. You can use playground **equipment** there. You can also practice sports. Maybe you'd like to have a picnic or study nature.

You can also do activities inside a park building called a **field house**. Maybe you like to play basketball on the courts at the park. You might like to take an art class in one of your park's classrooms.

Working together as a team helps park workers get a job done quicker.

Many people do a lot of different jobs in parks. They all work hard to give you a place to play that is fun and safe. Let's take a look at some park workers.

Create!

Draw a picture of your favorite park. Include drawings of all the things you like to do. Then draw each of the workers you usually see. How many workers did you draw?

Lifeguards are trained to rescue swimmers who are in trouble.

Park Workers

Does your local park have a soccer field or a basketball court? Maybe you went there with your **coach**. Coaches use parks for practices and games.

Some parks have swimming pools. Always listen to the **lifeguard**. He makes sure everyone in the park's pool stays safe. He rescues swimmers who are in trouble.

This worker is wearing special earmuffs.
They protect his ears from the loud noise of the
lawn mower.

Teachers work at the park, too. Some teach arts and crafts inside park buildings. Others lead fitness or nature classes in park buildings or outdoors. Some parks have summer camps. Camp **counselors** plan things for you to do at summer camp.

Groundskeepers trim trees and pick up garbage that has been left on the ground. They also plant gardens and mow grass. They help you enjoy nature by taking care of the beautiful trees and flowers that grow in the park.

Inspectors help make sure the playground equipment is safe to use.

Who helps you enjoy the playground? Playground **inspectors** check equipment such as swings and slides. Inspectors keep them safe for you to use. Other park workers repair broken playground equipment.

Park workers want you and your friends to have fun at the park.

Who is in charge of all these workers? A park **director** has this job. The park director usually works in an office. He plans park programs and figures out how to pay for them.

The park director also listens to people like you. He wants you to keep visiting the park and to be proud of it. In fact, all of the workers want the very same thing.

Some park workers decide where to plant flowers and other plants.

Do You Want to Work in a Park?

Would you like a job in a park someday? Start planning ahead!

Park workers enjoy being outside. Many are also good at helping people learn new things and have fun. It is easy for you to practice these skills.

Help workers keep your park clean. Always put your trash in the garbage can at the park.

Next time you are at the park, show your friends how to play your favorite sport. Tell them why it is important to take care of the park.

A park can be a great place to work. Learn as much as you can now. This is the best way to decide which job in the park is right for you!

GLOSSARY

coach (KOHCH) someone who trains a person or team to play a sport

counselors (KAUN-seh-luhrz) camp leaders

director (dih-REK-tuhr) person in charge of others who work for a group or organization

equipment (ee-KWIP-ment) objects such as slides and swings that people use on the playground

field house (FEELD HAUS) a park building that is sometimes used for indoor classes and sports games

groundskeeper (GROUNDZ-keep-uhr) a worker who cares for park grounds by keeping them clean and beautiful

inspectors (in-SPEK-tuhrz) people who check playground equipment to make sure it is safe and working the right way

lifeguards (LYFE-gardz) workers at a pool who protect swimmers

FIND OUT MORE

BOOKS

Cipriano, Jeri. *At the Park.* Mankato, MN: Yellow Umbrella Books, 2004.

Jones, Christianne C., and Matthew Skeens (illustrator). *The Lifeguard.* Minneapolis: Picture Window Books, 2006.

WEB SITES

Playground Safety for Kids!
www.kidchecker.org/tips.htm
Find out how to stay safe while having fun at a playground

Recreation and Fitness Worker
www.bls.gov/k12/sports04.htm
Learn more about recreation workers and what they do

INDEX

ABOUT THE AUTHOR

Katie Marsico is the author of more than 30 children's books. She lives in Elmhurst, Illinois, with her husband and two children. She would especially like to thank the staff of the Elmhurst Park District for helping her research this title.